Tramlink

Official Handbook

Michael Steward

John Gent

Colin Stannard

Capital Transport

D0537446

First published 2000

ISBN 185414 222 4

Published by Capital Transport Publishing
38 Long Elmes, Harrow Weald, Middlesex

Printed by CS Graphics, Singapore

© Capital Transport Publishing 2000

Photographic credits

Guy Brigden 11 Top

Capital Transport Publishing 14, 21 Bottom, 22, 25, 26, 58

B. J. Cross 20 Top, 24, 30, 38, 40 Bottom, 41 Top, 47, 49 Top

Croydon Public Libraries 5, 19 Top

G. Cunningham 10, 11 Centre, 12, 13, 15, 17, 20 Bottom,
        23 Bottom, 31, 35, 41 Bottom, 49 Bottom, 59, 60

John Gent 4, 9, 16, 18, 19 Bottom, 21 Top, 45

Brian Morrison 27 Top, 29, 39

Colin Stannard Cover, 1, 32, 33, 36, 40 Top, 42, 43 Top, 46, 50, 51, 61 Bottom

Michael Steward 43 Centre, 44 Top

The maps are by Mike Harris

FOREWORD

I have a golden memory from my early childhood. I remember distinctly travelling with my mother on an old London tramcar in South Croydon in 1951. I can just recall the tinted windscreen to keep the sun out of the driver's eyes.

From that encounter sprang a lifetime's interest in public transport. And an unshakeable affection for trams. I can hardly believe that they are coming back, not just to the London area, but to Croydon itself, which I know so well.

This book gives an excellent introduction to the system, which of course will be so much more advanced and 'consumer friendly' than those clanking old beasts that finished in the early fifties.

I am sure this handbook will be of great interest to enthusiast and non-enthusiast alike. Indeed, I hope it appeals to anyone intending to use Croydon Tramlink.

The present system could be just the start. May it not be too long before the trams are seen further afield. The future belongs to them!

Nicholas Owen,
Croydon, March 2000

CONTENTS

TRAMLINK'S PREDECESSORS

Croydon has an important place in the development of transport in Britain and it is appropriate that the first modern tramway in the south of England should be based in the town.

Croydon developed as a settlement just north of an important gap through the North Downs and charters for markets and fairs in the town were obtained from 1273 onwards. By the end of the eighteenth century it was a coaching centre and the largest town between London and the south coast, with a population of over 5000. Proposals for a canal between the Thames and Portsmouth had Croydon as its first objective. In the event, the canal only reached Croydon, opening in 1809. Meanwhile, in 1803, the Surrey Iron Railway, a horse drawn freight line, had opened from Wandsworth to Croydon. This was the first public railway in the world and by 1805 was extended to serve quarries at Merstham.

The canal was purchased by the London & Croydon Railway Company and closed in 1836 so that much of the alignment could be converted into a conventional railway line, which opened in 1839. This railway was responsible for many innovations including signalling, interlocking points, the first flyover and experiments with atmospheric traction. It merged into the London, Brighton and South Coast Railway in 1846.

More railways soon followed, including several of relevance to Tramlink. The Surrey Iron Railway closed in 1846 and part of its alignment was adopted by the Wimbledon and Croydon Railway from 1855. This line's section between Mitcham and Wandle Park subsequently became part of the Tramlink scheme. It is interesting to note that the alignment of the Tramlink street track, as it leaves the former rail route at Wandle Park, via Reeves Corner and Tamworth Road, closely follows the alignment of the canal company's tramroad. This once linked the Surrey Iron Railway's Pitlake terminus with the canal basin on the site now occupied by West Croydon station.

The South Eastern Railway built its own line from London to Croydon in 1864 via Lewisham. Inappropriately named the 'Mid Kent line', it terminated at Addiscombe Road. The Woodside and South Croydon Railway was a joint South Eastern and Brighton

A South Eastern and Chatham Railway steam train departs from Woodside towards Addiscombe in about 1910. Construction of Tramlink has involved the demolition of the platforms and canopies, but the station building on the overbridge remains.

Croydon Corporation tram 39 stands very close to the site of the new George Street tram stop, by Allders' side entrance. This was on 28th March 1927, the last day of operation of the original Addiscombe tram service.

Railways' venture from a junction with the 'Mid Kent' at Woodside to link with the newly opened Croydon, Oxted and East Grinstead Railway at Selsdon Road. Opening in 1885, this short line was never really successful, serving then mainly rural areas east of Croydon and suffering various periods of closure. It was nonetheless electrified in 1935 but final closure came on 13th May 1983 and most of the track was subsequently lifted. The section between Woodside Junction and Coombe Road is now part of Tramlink, as is the section of 'Mid Kent' between Elmers End and Blackhorse Lane. The last part of this, into Addiscombe, was closed after 31st May 1997, along with the Wimbledon–West Croydon line. Addiscombe station will, to some extent, be replaced by Tramlink's new Addiscombe stop adjacent to the site of Bingham Road station.

Croydon grew rapidly, with its population topping the 100,000 mark by the end of the century. In 1872 a Bill was presented to parliament for a London, Streatham and Croydon tramway, but this was rejected. In 1877, the Croydon Tramways Company proposed horse tram lines around the town, the first being from Thornton Heath to North End, opening on 3rd October 1879. In 1899, the Corporation purchased the lines and leased them to the British Electric Traction (BET) Company for operation. The main line between Norbury and Purley reopened using electric traction from 26th September 1901, with branches to Addiscombe, South Norwood and Thornton Heath High Street following in 1902. Some trams were owned by BET and some by Croydon Corporation, but in 1906 the Corporation terminated the BET lease. BET had by then set up a subsidiary company 'South Metropolitan Electric Tramways and Lighting Company', to construct lines to Sutton and Tooting as well as from South Norwood to Penge and Crystal Palace, which opened in 1906. By 1907, relationships between BET and Croydon Corporation had improved and a through running agreement was reached for joint running from the latter routes to West Croydon by both BET and Croydon Corporation trams. The Sutton and Tooting routes were not shared with Croydon and indeed connection was not permitted across the main road at West Croydon, so they terminated in Tamworth Road.

Similarly separated were the London County Council lines which reached Croydon's boundary at Norbury from the north in 1909, until the 6 inch gap between the two systems was finally bridged in 1926, and joint running eventually provided a direct through service from Purley to London.

Tramlink follows the original South Metropolitan (SMET) lines to Mitcham and Sutton along Tamworth Road, Croydon. In this 1931–32 view, the covered top London United tram (on loan to SMET) is rounding the curve into Lower Church Street towards Mitcham at what is now Reeves Corner Junction. SMET open top tram 9 waits to proceed towards Sutton, past the parish church.

Tramway abandonment started early in Croydon, with the closure of the Whitehorse Road route in 1913. In 1927, the route to Addiscombe saw its last tram because it was mainly single track with passing loops and there was insufficient finance available to renew the tracks on this line as well as to purchase new trams for the joint route to London. Tramlink has therefore restored trams to George Street and over East Croydon Station bridge after an absence of over 70 years!

In 1933, all the tramways in Croydon were absorbed by the London Passenger Transport Board, who abandoned the Penge route in favour of buses the following year. The companion route to Crystal Palace continued, gaining fame as the last route in London to be regularly worked by open top trams. It was replaced by trolleybuses in February 1936, which enabled it at last to be linked across West Croydon to the Sutton route (number 654), converted in 1935. The Tooting route was swallowed up by an extension of tram route 30 in December 1933, running all the way from College Park, Harlesden to West Croydon, which at 14 miles, was London's longest tram route. This route became trolleybus 630 from 12th September 1937, leaving trams on the north-south routes to soldier on for 14 more years thanks to a reprieve caused by the Second World War.

The peak hour frequency over the short section of single track beside the Whitgift Hospital in North End was some 38 trams per hour in each direction until the end of operation in Croydon. This came on 7th April 1951, when routes 16 and 18 from Purley to the Embankment were replaced by the 109 bus, and the local 42 tram, which branched off at Thornton Heath Pond, became bus 190. The 654 trolleybuses continued to serve Croydon until 1959, and the end of electric street traction in the Borough, at least for the time being, came when the 630 trolleybuses ran for the last time on 19th July 1960.

Tramlink therefore has an amazing collection of pioneering predecessors. With its advent, several streets will see trams for the first time, but as the previous paragraphs reveal, in several places it will appear to be a case of history repeating itself.

HOW TRAMLINK DEVELOPED

For many years, transport planners in London had been vexed by the question of how to serve adequately the township of New Addington. This was started as a new private housing area on open downland in the 1930s. Post-war it developed dramatically, much of it as overspill housing for inner Croydon residents. Following completion of the last major construction in the 1970s, population stood at 21,000. Residents were reliant on a bus service (albeit with an express operation) taking up to 45 minutes to get to East Croydon via a hilly route and both London Transport and the Borough clearly saw the need for something better.

In 1974–76, the Greater London Council carried out a study for an automatic people mover to link Croydon and New Addington, at a time when ideas of small, driverless tracked vehicles were in vogue, but this came to nothing. A decade later, London Transport and British Rail jointly carried out a study entitled 'Light Rail for London?', published in 1986. This scrutinised 40 possible opportunities for conversion of existing or disused rail lines to light rail operation as a way of increasing passenger usage and providing improved links. As well as construction of a line to New Addington, this featured the idea of connecting existing/former secondary rail routes across Croydon town centre by a street running line linking West and East Croydon. This report recommended a more comprehensive study of a Croydon network to define traffic potential and examine appropriate light rail technology.

This study was commissioned in 1987 and London Borough of Croydon officers participated. Its recommendations were that an initial network of three lines radiating from central Croydon to Wimbledon, Elmers End and New Addington would be technically and economically feasible and worthy of further investigation. Other local schemes were rejected due either to their need for common running with BR or lack of potential, and also to avoid developing too large a project.

A further joint Borough and LT Croydon Area Light Rail Study examined the local business community's perceptions of Croydon's problems and concluded that light rail would help Croydon to sustain its successful development as an alternative to costly and environmentally damaging road schemes. In this, its purpose differed from that of other recent light rail systems in that its aim was not regeneration. Croydon is Britain's tenth most populous town outside central London, with the largest concentration of office space and largest urban shopping centre in the south-east. Its main transport links have always been the radial north–south links with London, with east-west links being much poorer.

Workers and business customers come from far beyond Croydon borough and the car has been the automatic mode of choice for many. The adverse environmental effects on the quality of life, road safety, bus service reliability and access to car parking were recognised. This led to a consensus across the political spectrum on the then Conservative led Council that a transport strategy had to be developed to ensure that public transport could play an increasing role in satisfying mobility demands.

The 1987 study was updated in 1990 and recommendations made that design work and public consultation should be progressed. In June 1990 a final study was awarded to a consortium of consultants to carry out a detailed definition of a light rail scheme, and assessment of its environmental, economic and financial feasibility with a view to full public consultation on route options. The report from this study became the basis of the scheme jointly promoted by LT and the Borough, leading to the Croydon Tramlink Parliamentary Bill deposited in 1991.

Before the promoters could deposit the private Bill necessary to seek powers to construct the system, it was essential to attract strong local public support. An extensive information programme was embarked on prior to launching a formal public consultation process. At this stage, the name 'Tramlink' was coined to describe the function and purpose of the undertaking. The information and consultation process consisted of a range of leaflets distributed throughout the area, press advertising and detailed letters sent to all residents and businesses directly affected by the proposed routes. This was followed by a series of surgeries involving LT and Council representatives at various locations along the route. Displays were also set up in libraries and shopping centres. A particularly striking feature was the exhibition of a mock-up of a Sheffield Siemens tram in Queens Gardens, Croydon in April 1991.

The consultation was intended to be a meaningful process and one example of the success of this was the decision to remove the former rail embankment through Bingham Road station and construct the new line at street level. This was to avoid local residents having passengers looking down into their homes and it also enabled a more accessible stop facility.

Right In April 1991 a mock-up of a Sheffield Siemens tram was shown to the public in Queens Gardens, Croydon, as part of the public consultation process.

The Department of Transport was enthusiastic towards the scheme, although the way it could be funded was by no means clear at this stage.

A joint public/private venture was envisaged with LT and Croydon council as promoters, acquiring land, steering the Bill through Parliament and granting highway authority. Everything else from design and construction through to maintenance and operation would be the concern of a successful private bidder, likely to be a consortium of companies from all the various disciplines necessary. The Department of Transport insisted that the private sector should also be involved in the development of the project. As a result, private sector partners were chosen to join LT and LBC in a Project Development Group whose main tasks were to develop a system specification, financial forecasts and concession arrangements. The private sector's development costs were at risk at this stage, but would be reimbursed in the event of the project being implemented by others. Subsequently, in early 1995, it was decided to repay their costs, before the competition for the concession commenced.

Development work carried on between 1992 and 1994 to refine the scheme and amongst many achievements was the agreement to Merton Council's plan to extend Tramlink into platform 10 of Wimbledon station, instead of the remote terminus originally planned south of the station bridge. Also, at Beckenham Junction, it was agreed to change the alignment so that trams could terminate in the station forecourt. The Project Development Group developed a series of specifications for the system, designed to leave scope for initiative by the successful consortium in the competition to finance, develop, build, operate and maintain the complete system. One issue that came out of this stage was the uncertain but substantial cost of moving statutory undertakers' equipment from beneath the tram route. It was agreed that this risk should remain in the public sector to avoid deterring private sector partners.

In tandem with the Project Development Group, The Croydon Tramlink Bill was to work its way through the Parliamentary process. This was deposited in 1991 and sponsored as a private members procedure by David Congdon, Conservative MP for Croydon Central. It passed through the House of Lords and committee stage with little difficulty, but when it came to the Commons in 1993/4, its passage was somewhat rockier, mainly due to compensation levels proposed for affected householders. Some demands were eventually conceded and houses alongside the proposed flyover in Waddon New Road, Croydon were compulsorily purchased. This cleared the way for the third reading in the Commons in July 1994 and Royal Assent was granted on 21st July 1994. Interestingly,

Tramlink was the last transport project under the Parliamentary Bill procedure whereas the Surrey Iron Railway had been the first. Subsequent schemes would fall under the Transport and Works Act 1992 procedure.

Up to this time, Tramlink had been planned against a background in which deregulation of London's bus services was expected, which would have been likely to produce bus competition for Tramlink. However, in November 1993, the Conservative government decided to defer bus regulation in London, but proceed with privatisation of LT's bus companies.

London Transport wished Tramlink to be seen as part of an integrated transport network, and particularly to be part of the London-wide Travelcard and concessionary fares systems. This necessitated the service being covered by an agreement with LT under section 3(2) of the 1984 London Regional Transport Act. This gave LT the duty to control the level of fares and services.

In December 1994, Secretary of State for Transport Brian Mawhinney announced public funding for the Croydon Tramlink and Midlands Metro projects, provided they were advanced under the government's Private Finance Initiative. The amount, or proportion, of funding was not mentioned. The competition to finance, develop, build, operate and maintain the complete system was launched by Transport Minister Steven Norris on 30th May 1995, and an advertisement appeared in the Official Journal of the European Union to set the tendering process in motion. There was to be a first stage consisting of pre-qualification to establish competence and shortlist suitable candidates, followed by a detailed second stage that would be mainly judged on the lowest amount of government grant requested by bidders.

The pre-qualification competition produced eight applications, which were then slimmed down to four groups consisting of these partners:

Altram:	John Laing, Ansaldo Transporti and Serco Group.
Croydon Connect:	Tarmac, AEG, Transdev (the Project Development Group partners).
CT Light Rail Group:	GEC Alsthom, John Mowlem & Company, Welsh Water.
Tramtrack Croydon:	CentreWest Buses, Royal Bank of Scotland, Sir Robert McAlpine, Amey Construction, Bombardier Eurorail.

Bids had to be submitted in January 1996. An announcement was made in April 1996 that Tramtrack Croydon Ltd (TCL) had been granted preferred bidder status on the understanding that they would work with the promoters to reduce the cost of the scheme to a level acceptable to the government. During the following months, cost saving schemes agreed included the cutting back of the line at New Addington from the library to the health centre, and replacement of the proposed new tunnel at the top of Gravel Hill by a road crossing. Elsewhere, the amount of double track on the Wimbledon line was to be reduced. The ticket machines were downgraded to exclude magnetic coding capability and cheaper masts to support the overhead wires were chosen.

These and other economies enabled Steven Norris to announce on 22nd July 1996 that grant money was to be made available subject to satisfactory conclusion of negotiations. This was achieved on 25th November when a 99-year concession was awarded to TCL, with a predicted opening date of 4th November 1999. The government agreed a grant of £125 million towards the scheme, which included a substantial amount for LT to pay for all the statutory undertakers' works necessary before actual tramway construction could begin.

CONSTRUCTION PROGRAMME

A striking night-time vista of Croydon provides a backdrop as preparations are made to lift into position the main spans of the Wandle Park flyover on 25th April 1998.

Following the initial bid process TCL were named Preferred Bidder in April 1996. At that time the construction programme duration was set at 159 weeks with an anticipated start in the late spring of that year and a finish just over three years later.

Negotiating the final contract details took several months longer than expected. With each round of offer and counter-offer taking time, the start date inevitably went back. As the start moved towards the end of 1996 and, therefore, the end date closer to the millennium the pressure increased to shorten the programme. This further complicated the financial negotiations as each reduction in the overall duration required a re-casting of the cash flow forecast and a reconsideration of the costs.

Agreement was finally achieved in the early hours of Monday 25th November 1996 with a formal start date of the same day. The contract duration was set as 154 weeks to meet a planned opening of the system to fare paying passengers on 4th November 1999.

The revised programme did not differ significantly from the tender programme, but more overlap of activities was introduced to achieve the time saving required. The design programme commenced immediately after the start and ran for 18 months. During the first six months only utilities diversions and some accommodation works were scheduled to take place on site. Construction was set to commence in earnest in July 1997 and was intended to continue until March 1999. The final eight months were set aside for testing and commissioning of the system.

To replace the former flat junctions at Mitcham Junction Station, Tramlink has a separate stop parallel to the rail alignment, and the line to Sutton is crossed by the new flyover, which can be seen behind a Railtrack service unit. A Tramlink construction train sits on the westbound track.

Due to insufficient clearance under the road overbridge at Woodside, it was not possible to re-use the former rail platforms, and these had to be completely removed.

Utilities diversions, with an initial budget of £17m, started on 6th January 1997 and were substantially complete by August 1998. The risks associated with utilities diversions were retained by London Transport (LT) under the terms of the contract and these works were undertaken directly for LT. They in turn used Turner and Townsend Project Management to administer this element of the works.

Tramlink utilises former railway corridors for almost half of its length, the majority of which was in Railtrack use at the start of the project. As a condition of the Croydon Tramlink Act 1994 the tramway had to be fully separated from Railtrack infrastructure. This part of the contract, known as the Category A works, was undertaken by the TCL constructors under a supplementary agreement, the General Works Agreement, entered into with Railtrack. The works involved changes to permanent way, signalling, power supply and communications. In the design of the tramway, new structures were also required to grade-separate Tramlink from Railtrack at Mitcham Junction and at Wandle Park. The Category A works commenced on time in July 1997 following cessation of Railtrack services at the end of May, but it was quickly found that the extent of the changes needed and the improvements required to meet current Railtrack standards were in excess of that expected. As a result Category A works were not completed until July 1999, more than a year later than planned. With the co-operation of Railtrack, most significant delays were avoided by working around problems as they arose.

Left The former low rail overbridges in Lower Addiscombe Road and Bingham Road were removed following closure of the Woodside–Selsdon line in 1983. Rather than raise the embankment and replace the bridges, Tramlink completely removed the earthworks to ground level to facilitate a convenient tram stop here, between two level crossings.

Left At East Croydon Station, it was necessary to replace the early steel troughing of part of the overbridge by concrete spans, July 1998.

Right The former rail tunnels between Sandilands and Coombe Road were refurbished for their new purpose. North of the tunnels, a new sloping cutting was constructed up to road level to enable the new tracks to reach Addiscombe Road. In March 1999, the curves of the rails towards Lloyd Park (through the tunnel) and Addiscombe (foreground) were being positioned.

Aside from early accommodation works, construction of the Tramlink infrastructure commenced on four fronts, three corresponding to the branches of the system and the fourth dealing with the central Croydon street running area. This latter section formed the critical path for the civil engineering phase of the project as it was constrained by the need to divert utilities first and by traffic management restrictions imposed by the London Borough of Croydon (LBC) to prevent traffic grid-lock.

To undertake the construction programme, the two civil engineering members of the Tramtrack consortium, Sir Robert McAlpine and Amey Construction, formed a Construction Joint Venture (CJV). Amongst other risks, CJV carried the design approval risk; under several sections of the Croydon Tramlink Act 1994, a variety of third parties had rights of approval over specific aspects of the scheme. The most significant of these third parties was undoubtedly LBC but other authorities, utilities and interested parties also had an input. These approvals proved harder to get than had been anticipated and whilst the work started on time it was only in a limited way. After a while approvals were prioritised and were generally received 'just in time' for work to proceed. Delays, for a variety of reasons did, however, accumulate and the main infrastructure was completed in July 1999, three months later than the planned finish. The sequence of construction had been significantly changed to ensure the timely delivery of key sections to the testing and commissioning team.

Tram delivery was planned on a manufacturing timetable. The Croydon trams are essentially a proven design already in use in Cologne, Germany but lengthened by about 1.5m. At the outset there was, therefore, a high level of certainty regarding build outputs. The design had to be modified to meet UK safety requirements, so the first tram was built for type approval following extensive discussions with the approving authority, Her Majesty's Railway Inspectorate (HMRI). Subsequent vehicles were batch-produced using production line techniques. At the outset the first tram was scheduled for delivery on 15 September 1998 and the first tram duly arrived on that date. The second tram was delivered a month later with further trams delivered at increasing frequency until one was delivered every two weeks. All 24 trams had been delivered to the Therapia Lane depot complex by June 1999 in line with the Contract Programme.

Several roads had to be re-aligned at Tramlink crossings, including Kent Gate Way, Addington and the entrances to the adjacent park.

At Elmers End terminus, Tramlink uses the former bay platform, in which the track has been raised to allow the platform height to remain level with the adjacent Connex platform. Nescafé advertising tram 2533 stands at the buffer stops during a training run on 20th October 1999.

With the delivery of the first tram, dynamic testing and commissioning could commence. The 'test track' for proving of vehicles and systems was intended to be the section between Wimbledon Station and Wandle Park. Construction delays led to a phased opening of the test track starting with Beddington Lane to Ampere Way. This was followed by an extension from Ampere Way to Wandle Park and then north-west from Beddington Lane to Phipps Bridge. Approval to run into Wimbledon Station was obtained in April 1999 following submissions to Railtrack on electro-magnetic compatibility. By mid-June 1999 the street running section of central Croydon was energised, followed closely by the entire New Addington branch. This, in turn, was followed by energisation of the leg to Elmers End. Prolonged Category A works and difficult access along the parallel running section between Birkbeck and Beckenham Junction led to this being the last section to be energised, in late July 1999. Test running on the Wimbledon branch was completed to the satisfaction of LT and TCL at the end of October 1999, but technical problems dashed hopes of beginning passenger services before the end of that year.

Above A road-rail vehicle was used for gauging runs over some sections of the system prior to energisation. On 15th August 1999 tight clearances near Beckenham Junction were being tested.

Left As part of the commissioning of Tramlink it was necessary to undertake various exercises with the emergency services. A simulated tram/bus accident was arranged in Wellesley Road, Croydon, on 11th July 1999.

A complicated track layout at Reeves Corner junction includes some interlaced track in Church Street, designed to avoid a point mechanism in the middle of a road junction.

TRACKWORK

The trackwork inherited from Railtrack was of a variety of forms and in a range of conditions. The contract allowed for a proportion of the existing track to be refurbished and reused. 8km of the track was refurbished from the 16km or so inherited from Railtrack at the start of the scheme, with a further 1km reused in the stabling at the depot. 5.4km is embedded rail in track slab construction with the remainder flat bottom rail on pre-cast concrete sleepers on track ballast. The trackwork was installed by Jarvis Rail under a major subcontract.

Off street the new track supplied generally consists of S49 (49kg per one metre length) section flat-bottom rail secured with Vossloh pattern clips to pre-stressed concrete Monobloc sleepers. Outside of central Croydon the track is conventional with rails on sleepers bedded on a minimum of 150mm of ballast.

For the street sections, after examining the track forms used in Sheffield, Manchester and to a lesser extent Birmingham, followed by design work and prototype testing, a reinforced concrete track slab was selected with embedded rails. Grooved rail of either type Ri59, with wider flangeway, on tight radii, or Ri60 elsewhere, is embedded into slots saw-cut into the concrete track slab. It is secured in cold-curing polymer, which provides electrical and vibration insulation from the reinforced concrete track slab, and holds the rail to gauge. The detailed method of finishing depends on whether a section is shared with road traffic, as that requires a more durable finish than where only trams run. At highway crossings on plain track sections, the S49 plain rail is run straight across with a separate piece of sheet section bolted on to provide a flangeway instead of grooved rail and this method is also used on East Croydon bridge and George Street over the underpass, where the deeper section Ri60 rail cannot be used. At vibration sensitive locations, at the Almshouses in central Croydon and at Parkway Health Centre near Addington terminus, the trackslab was cast on resilient matting. In the tunnels ballast matting was used.

Pointwork was supplied by Voest-Alpine (VAE) of Austria and is equipped with operating mechanisms by Hanning and Kahl. Although there are, excluding the depot, 48 sets of points on the system only nine sets, where route selection is required, are motorised; all other points are sprung as movement is always in the trailing direction. The motorised points at junctions are set by local equipment which communicates with an approaching tram and reacts to the destination code which has been preset on the transponder fitted underneath the tram. Emergency crossovers are manually set by tram drivers using point levers kept in the cabs of each tram. Indicators are provided at all points normally used in the facing direction to advise the tram drivers that the route is correctly set.

The track consists of a mixture of twin and single sections. The single line sections on the Wimbledon branch are designed to be at locations where the inbound and outbound trams will not cross, provided the trams are within a minute of their timetabled position, so no delays are incurred. The passing points on the Birkbeck to Beckenham section were effectively fixed by physical constraints so the timetable had to be worked around them.

Right An interesting comparison is enabled by these two photographs of tram lines in George Street, Croydon, alongside the historic Whitgift Hospital of 1596. The first view shows the removal of the original Addiscombe route tracks on 6th August 1927. The companion photograph from the same viewpoint on 1st December 1998 shows Tramlink rails being laid on a very similar alignment 71 years later.

Prior to the laying of ballast, matting was placed in position on the non-street sections. In the Addington Hills, construction involved new cuttings and embankments.

In total there are just under 52 track kilometres making up the 28km system. The Wimbledon and Beckenham branches are a mixture of twin track and single track. Croydon town centre consists of a single track 'loop' with twin track extending to Sandilands in the east. The New Addington branch is all twin track with the exception of a short length around the Health Centre on Parkway, just before the terminus at New Addington.

The track lengths on each section are as follows:

Branch	branch km	track km
Wimbledon	9.4	15.8
Depot		3.4
Beckenham	7.0	10.6
New Addington	7.6	16.4
Central Croydon	4.2	5.5

Track speeds range from 80kph in the rural sections to as little as 15kph in the town.

The first grooved rails were laid in Addiscombe Road, Croydon, on 25th June 1998.

Street rails are held in place in their cut grooves by polymer. To enable this to cure, shelters were used in some locations.

The method of joining grooved rail (nearest the camera) to shallower section plain track with separate flangeway is demonstrated in this view at East Croydon. The shallower plain rail is used here because of the restricted clearances.

Street track not normally used by other road traffic is generally finished with block paving, as shown in this view of the George Street/Wellesley Road junction, where the separate central Croydon routeings meet.

THE TRAMS

No.2544 displays the sleek lines of Croydon's trams.

From the start of the project, it was made clear that all technical aspects should be 'tried and tested', in order to keep costs of the project within a tight budget.

The rolling stock is always a major element of the cost of any rail-based project and the promoters were keen to see bids from established manufacturers utilising tram designs already in operation elsewhere.

The Tramtrack Croydon Ltd consortium's vehicle manufacturing member was Bombardier Transportation. Bombardier is a world-wide supplier of transport equipment, including aircraft, rail vehicles, trams, snowmobiles and water craft. In Europe, it owns established tram constructors BN in Belgium, Vevey in Switzerland and BWS in Austria.

London Transport's specification left it to bidders to determine tram passenger capacity based on required provision on various sections of the network, but it did state that at least 30% of the passenger capacity had to be seated. The vehicles had to be accessible by wheelchairs, with 2 wheelchair spaces provided. Maximum tram length, dictated by road space, could be up to 45 metres.

To meet the specification, Bombardier put forward a design based on the K4000 articulated tram that was being supplied to Cologne from 1995. Following the U6 type for Vienna this was the second low-floor tram model to be produced by BWS at their Vienna factory, and so far 120 have been built and delivered. In Cologne, the trams had proved to be highly reliable and relatively few technical modifications were necessary to make the model suitable for Croydon.

All trams were delivered from Vienna by lowloader, the final leg usually being on a Monday evening from Dartford Dock to Croydon via the M25 and A22. At Purley on 7th June 1999, the last tram, No.2553, is escorted the wrong way round the one-way system to avoid a tight turn.

Below On arrival at the depot, trams were gently rolled from the lowloader onto a track. The first tram (No.2530) is being unloaded on 14th September 1998. It was then pushed into the depot building.

The very first run of a new Croydon tram occurred on the morning of 8th October 1998 when unnumbered 2530 undertook slow speed runs near Therapia Lane.

On 16th June 1999 No.2535 performed the first powered run on the street sections of the system, escorted by police motorcycles.

The tram has two almost 'mirror-image' sections connected by a short central section over a central bogie, with articulations between each part. Overall length is 30.1 metres and width 2.65 metres, with each end slightly tapered. The low floor area of 400mm height, with an entrance height of 350mm from the top of the rail, extends over 76% of the passenger compartment. There is a single step up from this area to a higher floor section over the power bogie at each end, each containing 16 seats. In total there are 70 seats in the vehicle and a further 138 standing passengers can be accommodated at a spacing of 4 passengers per square metre. A position for one wheelchair is sited between the first two sets of offside doors in each section. On each side of the tram are four 1305mm wide doorways with sliding plug type doors. Internally, the trams are finished in a light grey colour scheme, with blue seat covers and yellow handrails.

Croydon trams have an identical cab at each end. The access door is on the offside.

The drivers' cabs have exterior inward-opening doors to the offside, the same position as in Cologne. They also have an opening door into the saloon. The driver is provided with a comfortable seat sited slightly to the nearside, with the main controls to the left hand. Each cab is equipped with radio and electrical equipment necessary for service control purposes.

The electrical equipment and running gear is supplied by Kiepe Elektrik of Düsseldorf in Germany. Four 120Kw 3-phase asynchronous motors are fitted to the two powered two-axle bogies towards the ends of the tram and there is an unpowered independent four-wheel bogie under the central articulation. Bogies have rubber/metal primary suspension with coil spring secondary suspension. Sanders are fitted to each of the eight powered wheels. An anti-slip and slide system is provided.

Three different brake systems are fitted to the trams: an electric regenerative service brake, an hydraulic/mechanical disc brake and a magnetic track brake.

Current at 750V DC is collected from the overhead by a Shunk type pantograph fitted above the inner pair of doors on one section of the tram. Low voltage equipment on the tram is at 24V DC.

The tram is capable of a maximum speed of 80 kmph (50 mph) and can accelerate at up to 1.2m/s^2. Normal braking rate at 80 kmph is 1.3m/s^2 although in an emergency this is 2.75m/s^2.

The trams are numbered in a sequence from 2530 to 2553. These numbers follow on directly from the highest numbered previous London tram.

The first tram was completed in Vienna by June 1998 and then underwent exhaustive testing at the BWS plant and on a test track in Vienna, so that it would be ready for operation on arrival in the UK. Tram 2530 was conveyed by road from Vienna, crossing to England from Vlissingen, Holland on a ferry to Dartford in Kent, where it arrived on 13th September 1998. It was brought to Croydon via the M25 and A22, arriving at Therapia Lane depot in the late evening of 14th September. The remaining 23 trams were delivered in sequence between September 1998 and June 1999.

Above left On each side of the tram there are four pairs of doors, largely made of glass but with heavy steel frames.

Above The centre, unpowered bogie supports a short central body section, joined to the two end sections by concertina bellows.

Above There is level access across the central articulation unit. The end sections, over the powered bogies, are the only parts of the interior that have steps.

Right In each end section of the tram there is a designated area for wheelchairs, which is available for pushchairs and standing passengers when not required for wheelchairs.

Tramlink ⊖

TRAMLINK'S ROUTES DESCRIBED

Manchester Metrolink, the country's first new generation tram system, was largely routed over existing rail alignments, new construction being limited to street track in Manchester city centre. Sheffield, on the other hand, was mostly new construction, much of it on mixed usage highway, with private right of way only on the Meadowhall line and various reserved track sections. West Midlands too, is largely on former rail alignment except for some street operation in Wolverhampton.

Croydon Tramlink could be described as having elements of all the preceding systems, with extensive use of former rail alignments on both sides of Croydon, street track in the town centre area (mostly restricted usage), but with major new construction of private right of way at South Norwood Country Park and on the New Addington route. The latter is a completely new reserved track tramway and could also be described as the most spectacular tram ride in the country (with due respect to Sheffield and Crich tram museum) with steep gradients through woodland and open country, roadside running and tunnels on the old rail alignment.

Fanning out from Croydon town centre, Tramlink runs to four separate terminals, one to the west and three on the east side of Croydon. All four sections make some use of previous rail alignments, either those in use currently or recently or disused since 1983. The previous history of these lines is related in the first chapter, dealing with Tramlink's predecessors.

Coming from the west, the Wimbledon–Croydon line joins the rest of the system at Reeves Corner junction, on the town centre one-way loop. All routes run from this point to Sandilands junction, about one kilometre east of Croydon, the two parts of the loop rejoining at the George Street/Wellesley Road intersection in the town centre. At Sandilands trams turn sharp left for the Beckenham and Elmers End routes and right for New Addington. The short Elmers End line diverges from the Beckenham route at Arena junction, about four kilometres from Croydon.

South Norwood Country Park is the only part of the Beckenham branch to be 'new build'. The New Addington branch is 'new build' from Larcombe Close to New Addington terminus. It was, therefore, on these sections that the major earthworks were required. The total quantity moved amounted to about 120,000m³, not a large quantity by earth moving standards but big enough to cause problems in an urban environment. The vertical alignment was designed to produce a small excess for disposal into landscape thus keeping as much of the material on site as possible and minimising the number of truck movements into and out of the site. In the end the surplus was used in reducing embankment side slopes, in an improvement to playing fields in South Norwood Country Park and in an area of Heathfield Park where it was used to conceal Tramlink, reducing its impact.

The scheme impacted on over 80 existing structures, all of which had to be assessed and, where necessary, modified for Tramlink operation. Five existing bridges were re-decked for Tramlink use, including one span of the Railtrack structure carrying George Street East at East Croydon Station. New structures ranged from the two crossings of Railtrack at Mitcham Junction and Wandle Park to numerous small retaining walls.

The Tramlink platform at
Wimbledon is part of the
Railtrack station. Only one
tram at a time can be
accommodated at this
terminus.

Wimbledon–Croydon line

This almost exclusively follows the Wimbledon–West Croydon railway line, from which
the service was withdrawn in May 1997. It is a fairly straight and level alignment, following
the original alignment of the historic Surrey Iron Railway along the plain of the River
Wandle for about half of its length. The only divergences from the rail route are at
Mitcham Junction station where Tramlink takes a different alignment to the south of the
Railtrack platforms and uses a flyover to segregate itself from Railtrack lines, and at
Wandle Park where it again rises over a new flyover to replace the former flat rail junction.
The main line is also re-aligned where it passes Therapia Lane depot.

The former rail route was always regarded as a backwater and supported a minimal
service in later years. Apart from connecting the major centres of Wimbledon and
Croydon, it had few stations of any importance and no new stations were ever added to
serve new housing estates that grew up alongside the route in the last 30 years. Whilst
this may seem unpromising territory for a high frequency tram, new stops serving the
Phipps Bridge high density housing area, new housing in the Therapia Lane area and the
vast Purley Way and Valley Park retail area all present new traffic. In addition, the
attraction of a frequent end-to-end service, linking Wimbledon to East Croydon Station
in less than half-an-hour, will revolutionise orbital travel in south-west London.

Tramlink starts from a single line at platform 10 on the east side of Wimbledon Station.
In order to make use of the existing full-height rail platform, the Tramlink track has been
raised on concrete beams to bring the tram entrances level with the platform. The far
end of the platform has been retained as a dead end bay by Railtrack for use by reversing
trains, and this has restricted the length available, so that it is not possible for two of the
30 metre trams to be accommodated at the same time, in the event of operating difficulties.
At Wimbledon, passengers have to enter through the main railway entrances accessing
the overbridge and as ticket operated barriers were fitted in 1998, Tramlink passengers
have to be issued with magnetic strip tickets.

Departing from Wimbledon station under the wide bridge that supports Wimbledon Hill Road and shops on both sides of it, the single track then veers away to the left at the site of a former crossover with the straight ahead Railtrack lines; the lines are now completely separate. From this point the alignment widens out and there is sufficient width for two running tracks as well as, immediately on the left, a siding. This is designed to permit a spare tram to be shunted clear of the running lines. The lines continue to curve round into the first stop at Dundonald Road, just before the level crossing. This is a completely new stop and has side platforms. As with all major road crossings on the route, traffic signals have replaced the previous lifting barriers.

The double track straightens out and continues the short distance to cross the main A238 Kingston Road at a complicated and busy three-way road junction at which trams should receive priority. Beyond the crossing is Merton Park stop which is on the site of the former station and junction with the Merton Abbey branch (which finally closed in 1972, having lost its passenger service in 1929).

From here, the track is generally straight for a considerable distance. Double track continues alongside a sports ground on the north side to Morden Road stop, in a shallow cutting beneath an overbridge carrying the A24 road. Previously, there was a single platform on single track, which carried the suffix 'Halt' for many years. This stop is unfortunately the nearest the trams get to the important transport interchange at Morden Underground station, over 1.5 kms away.

Excellent interchange with rail services is provided at Mitcham Junction. A driver training run departs towards Beddington Lane.

After this stop, the track becomes single as it runs alongside the extensive Mordenhall Park on the south side. Two bridges over the River Wandle and a side channel are crossed before the large housing area of Phipps Bridge appears on the north side, which was ignored by the former BR trains. The track becomes double again at the new island platform stop located by a footpath into the estate; there is no road access at this stop. Double track continues the short distance to the new centre platform Belgrave Walk stop, intended to serve the eastern end of the housing, and this also has no road access. In earlier days there were extensive rail sidings on the south side of the line.

After Belgrave Walk, the double track carries on for a distance, but is then interlaced for a short distance as it enters a cutting with retaining walls. Failure of the north side wall in the 1960s resulted in concrete blocks being installed on the eastbound line to support it and the adjacent buildings; removal of these would have been extremely difficult. After the bridge under London Road, the track becomes double for the Mitcham stop which has side platforms in a shallow cutting. This was a relatively busy station in BR days and the original road level buildings (now listed) survive in private use as offices. An interesting coincidence is that a lane adjacent to the alignment here is named Tramway Path, which refers to the original use of the alignment by the Surrey Iron Railway from 1803.

Below No.2540 heads across one of the bridges over the River Wandle between Phipps Bridge and Morden Road.

Below right Interlaced track is used for a short section near Mitcham stop where the width of the former rail alignment is restricted by concrete blocks reinforcing the original cutting wall.

A tram leaves the single line at Beddington Lane and is approaching the tram stop. The former Beddington Lane railway station had a single platform on the site of the track to the right. The track on the left is the old railway track re-used.

Single track is resumed after the Mitcham stop loop, and on the south side runs alongside the Willow Lane industrial estate, which may ultimately be served by an additional stop. After the bridge under Willow Lane, the Connex South Central Victoria–Sutton line comes in from the left and there was formerly a double track junction here. To avoid this, the Tramlink single line moves to the right and runs through a spare arch in the bridge under Carshalton Road. It then squeezes behind the London-bound Railtrack platform and branches into a loop with side platforms, at Tramlink's Mitcham Junction stop, which is parallel to the existing Railtrack platforms on their south-west side. The station entrance and booking hall are on the north-east side, Sutton-bound platform, and an existing footbridge gives access to the London-bound platform and, through an arch in the wall, to Tramlink's platforms. A new pedestrian access and substation are on the south side.

The platforms are situated on a slight grade and, immediately on leaving the stop, the track becomes single as eastbound trams have to rise up to the imposing flyover that carries the track over the Railtrack lines as they curve to the right towards Hackbridge. Mitcham Junction flyover is a single span steel plate girder of 'half through' design on a high skew crossing the Railtrack lines to Hackbridge. It differs from conventional railway bridges in that it uses pre-cast concrete units to form the deck rather than steel troughing. The bridge sits on reinforced concrete bank seats which in turn rest on reinforced soil approach embankments. Reinforced soil was chosen for its speed of construction and because virtually no temporary works were required adjacent to Railtrack operations. The steel girders were lifted in to position in one unit using a 400 tonne capacity mobile crane during a weekend possession of the railway line on 15th November 1997.

To the north of this flyover there was previously a flat junction between the lines to Croydon and Hackbridge. Trams then regain the former alignment, which runs dead straight across the windswept Mitcham Common on a single track until it passes industrial units prior to regaining double track as it enters the Beddington Lane stop. As at Morden Road, this was previously a single platform on single track, also being described as a 'Halt' at one time, serving an isolated community and the industrial sites. Tramlink has replaced this with a side platform stop on double track which continues on from here to the next physical constraint at Wandle Park flyover.

No.2534 emerges from under Roman Way and approaches the ramp up to Wandle Park flyover *en route* to Wimbledon.

The curve of the Wandle Park flyover forms the background as No.2530 bends round on its journey towards Wimbledon.

Crossing Beddington Lane under traffic signals protection, the tracks then approach the Therapia Lane depot, which occupies a site 700 metres long but only 80 metres wide. To give sufficient space for the depot, the line diverges from the straight BR alignment to run alongside the north side of the depot, separated by a wire fence. All of this area at one time contained railway sidings to serve Croydon power station and other industries. At the western end of the depot is a crossover and a single track access line, so that trams to Wimbledon can enter service here. Short side platforms are provided alongside the depot for use by staff only.

Reaching the eastern end of the depot, the line curves around to regain the former alignment again and passes the main depot entrance, which is used by the majority of trams going into service and all those entering the depot; this is so that they can access the washing machine which is located alongside the depot building. A crossover provides access from the depot to the eastbound line and permits trams finishing service from Wimbledon to reverse into the depot.

Shortly after the crossover, Therapia Lane stop is reached and, like all remaining stops on this section, it possesses side platforms. Soon after, a further similar stop named Ampere Way is reached; this road name commemorates the site's earlier occupation by Croydon power station and evidence of this is still present in the prominent shape of the two chimneys, which have been retained as a landmark for the adjacent IKEA superstore, with its huge car park. The line now goes under the A23 Purley Way before passing the original site of Waddon Marsh rail station, which existed to serve housing on the north of the line. The new tram stop of the same name is located 200 metres further on to provide a more convenient location central to the Purley Way retail area, behind a Sainsbury superstore.

Passing Croydon's gasholders, the line continues to a new stop at Wandle Park, which appears on the left hand side as the track curves to the left. The two-track section becomes single after the stop in order to climb up to the Wandle Park flyover, which was erected to separate the line from the Sutton–West Croydon Railtrack line. This curved viaduct brings Tramlink round parallel to the railway lines, which it then descends to run alongside for a short distance.

Wandle Park Flyover was a difficult structure to design and build. Firstly there was a Parliamentary undertaking to consult with local residents on the form of the structure. Secondly the alignment was very constrained by a road, a public park, the Sutton to West Croydon railway, and the existing West Croydon to Wimbledon railway corridor which Tramlink took over. Thirdly the horizontal and vertical alignment were driven by the vehicle characteristics with certain combinations of horizontal and vertical curvature not permitted. Fourthly ground conditions were poor, with 10m–15m of terrace gravel and alluvium overlying chalk. Finally there were issues with utilities including sewers crossing the alignment and an electricity substation which had to be retained.

The combination of vertical and horizontal alignments coupled with the choice of pre-cast beams over the railway led to a structure with potentially dubious aesthetics. To mitigate this the parapets were constructed in-situ and followed a flowing curve. On the Waddon New Road side the in-situ deck construction also followed a curve. The structure landed onto reinforced soil embankments at each end, selected here purely for the simplicity of construction adjacent to a live railway. The design of the resulting wall alongside Waddon New Road was not, however, acceptable to the residents of Waddon New Road and Rectory Grove. After protracted discussion and rework the bridge was eventually extended from three to five spans which retained views to the park opposite from Rectory Grove and nearby properties on Waddon New Road. What remained of the wall was brick clad.

The awkward location of the Wandle Park flyover is demonstrated by this view with the park in the background. A three-span steel truss structure was originally proposed for this site, but a study undertaken at the award of contract quickly led to the bridge being of concrete design on noise grounds.

Back at ground level, Tramlink leaves the rail corridor through a paved area designed to discourage pedestrian access and runs alongside Waddon New Road, under the Roman Way road bridge. At this point it executes a 140 degree turn to the right and resumes two-line operation, before entering the street for the first time. This is in Cairo New Road and eastbound trams only then have a side platform stop, on the pavement, at Reeves Corner (Wimbledon bound trams have an equivalent stop the other side of the junction in Church Street). Original plans did not include a stop here, but it was decided to provide one, as passengers coming from the Wimbledon direction and requiring the southern part of the shopping centre would otherwise have been taken some distance out of their way, to West Croydon. Shortly after the stop is Reeves Corner junction, so named after the sprawling, long-established furniture shop that is a landmark at this point. Here, the Wimbledon line joins the town centre loop.

Croydon town centre

In the initial stage of planning Tramlink, London Transport wished to pursue tram operation along North End, Croydon's principal shopping thoroughfare. This had originally been the trunk tram and bus route through Croydon, but several unfortunate incidents in the 1980s, when it had become a bus and pedestrian mall, had led Croydon Council to ban buses. It was felt in Croydon that reopening the now fully pedestrianised road to public transport would be unacceptable politically and so another route had to be found.

This proved to be awkward, as ideally trams should have served both West Croydon and the heart of the shopping/commercial centre. The solution that emerged was something of a compromise with this as it was agreed that single track operation would be possible in George Street (West) and Church Street, albeit not passing West Croydon. Thus, the westbound through route goes this way, but the return route is via Tamworth Road, West Croydon, Station Road and Wellesley Road. This unfortunately meant that trams to and from Wimbledon could not serve the same town centre points in both directions.

After a fast run along the median strip in Wellesley Road, No.2532 crosses over to the nearside prior to entering Wellesley Road tram stop.

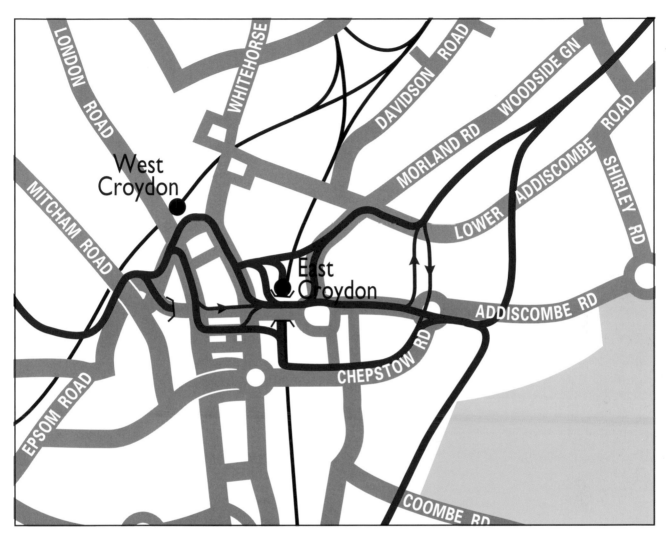

Early planning of the route of Tramlink through central Croydon looked at various options including running into East Croydon station and an underpass at Crown Hill. The southern leg at this stage was directed towards Sanderstead.

Continuing on from Reeves Corner junction, where trams on the loop from the east can either proceed north-west into Cairo New Road towards Wimbledon or fork right into Tamworth Road to a junction with trams from Wimbledon, the single track loop proceeds up Tamworth Road to West Croydon. This is one of the few stretches previously used by trams, prior to 1937. The eastbound track is shared by buses, with a separate lane for cars as far as the Drummond car park. There is currently no tram stop on this section, although buses can pull into bus bays, but during 1999, plans for an additional stop to serve a proposed extended shopping centre were put forward by a developer. At the top of Tamworth Road, the road curves to the right alongside a pavement cantilevered over the adjacent railway cutting. The major West Croydon road junction is then crossed under traffic signal control, to enter Station Road, still shared with buses. The West Croydon tram stop is located on the left hand pavement opposite the bus station and alongside the rear wall of West Croydon Station, although the entrance is several hundred metres away in London Road. It is hoped that eventually an entrance to the station can be made by the tram stop to give excellent interchange between three transport modes.

The tram route now reaches the complex signalled road junction with Wellesley Road, the main through route in the town centre. The trams have to sweep sharply round to the right to gain a central reservation in the median strip, and after passing through a signalled U turn, there is an opportunity to pick up speed along a straight section flanked by tall office blocks and car parks. This ends opposite the major Whitgift shopping centre where, protected by traffic signals, the single track has to cross to the nearside kerb of Wellesley Road to access the pavement stop carrying that name. Shortly after the stop, the road junction with George Street is reached and the route turns left to rejoin the westbound track. It was originally intended to have a connection here to George Street (West), but this was dropped before the tendering process commenced.

Following the westbound section of the Croydon loop from this point, the single track crosses the wide George Street/Wellesley Road intersection to enter the narrow western part of George Street. This street is the same width as when it last previously carried trams in 1927 and there is mostly insufficient space for two tracks. The George Street stop is fitted in tightly, on the pavement adjacent to Allders Mall, on the offside of the trams. Immediately on leaving this stop, the track has to veer to the left to avoid the Whitgift Hospital of 1596, one of Croydon's most historic buildings, and the track here has special underlay to protect against vibration. It then forks slightly to the right to cross the now pedestrianised North End shopping street and immediately plunges down the 9% grade in Crown Hill, also pedestrianised. This section calls for extreme care on the part of drivers.

At the foot of the short sharp grade, Church Street is reached and trams share the narrow carriageway of this with other traffic. This is also a busy shopping street, mostly of smaller shops, and slow running is necessary. The Church Street stop is located on the offside pavement just beyond Old Palace Road. Soon after this, points split the line into

Above left No.2538 on the interlaced section at Reeves Corner junction, where the loop track diverges from the straight-ahead Wimbledon line.

Above The rear of No.2535 at Church Street stop. At this point, Church Street becomes a tram-only thoroughfare.

Running on the single track leading to George Street, tram 2535 travels along the middle of Wellesley Road.

a section of interlaced track leading to Reeves Corner junction, so completing the town centre loop. This interlacing is to avoid point blades in the roadway.

Resuming the eastbound journey at the junction of Wellesley Road and George Street (East), the double track runs on paved track along what used to be the northern side of the former dual carriageway in George Street, the south side now being a two-way road. After the junction with Dingwall Road, the road rises up to the East Croydon bridge and at this point the lines split into three tracks through the stop for the station, the busiest on the system. The central track is accessible from both directions and is used by trams in the peak direction flow to reduce delays caused by heavy passenger movements. It can also be used if there is a need to terminate a tram here, or to hold an out of service tram. The north side track has a side platform forming part of the pavement in front of the station building, whilst the other two tracks share an island platform.

After a detailed search through the Railtrack archives at Waterloo, followed by inspection and assessment, the existing bridge at East Croydon Station was found to consist of no fewer than 17 elements. The complex structure had been added to and modified over the years ranging from a 1960s concrete bridge on the south side to original Victorian brick arches. The part of the structure carrying Tramlink consisted of two spans of early steel construction and two spans of brick arches. Analysis showed that the western span, in early steel, was incapable of carrying Tramlink loading and the next span was close to its limit. The western span was replaced with pre-cast concrete beams during a series of weekend possessions of the busy railway lines beneath for demolition, placing beams and casting of the concrete infill. The other span was dealt with by removing the old trough infill and replacing with lightweight concrete for which no possessions were required. The whole structure was then re-waterproofed and the track slab constructed over. Finally the spaces between track slabs were infilled with further lightweight concrete.

Approaching East Croydon, it is necessary for westbound trams to stop before crossing the taxi exit road prior to entering the tram stop.

After leaving East Croydon, two tracks continue along the north side of the former roundabout past the imposing NLA tower office block and then cross Cherry Orchard Road into Addiscombe Road. The next section consists of double track in a curving residential road only just wide enough for it, and other traffic is restricted to buses and access vehicles. Lebanon Road stop is located on this section and because of the number of side roads close together and provision of bus stop bays, the two pavement platforms have to be staggered.

After Lebanon Road stop, the street track continues to the major road intersection with Chepstow Road, which is part of the busy A232 red route. Until tramway construction, there was a roundabout here, but this has been replaced by a signal controlled crossing to provide sufficient capacity. The tracks now move to a side reservation on the south side of Addiscombe Road, passing a large block of flats, in front of which is a trailing crossover for emergency use. The line then moves away from the road and enters Sandilands stop at Woodbury Close, built on the site of some of the few houses it was necessary to demolish for construction. This is a side platform stop.

With Sandilands stop in the background, No.2553 is about to leave reserved track and cross the busy Chepstow Road intersection before joining the street track in Addiscombe Road.

Above The track along Addiscombe Road, Croydon, has a very traditional feel to it. No.2543 passes Lebanon Road stop on a trial run in September 1999.

Below The Beckenham and Addington lines join at Sandilands Junction, which is situated in the new, graded cutting constructed to access the former rail alignment between Coombe Road and Addiscombe.

Croydon–Beckenham and Elmers End line

Immediately after leaving Sandilands, the nature of the system changes dramatically as trams descend to the junction splitting the Beckenham and New Addington lines. The tracks turn sharply through 90° to both north and south to gain the former Woodside–Selsdon rail alignment, at this point in a deep cutting.

The northern line immediately passes under the original Addiscombe Road bridge. Gradually, the cutting gives way to an embankment and this formerly carried on rising to cross Bingham Road and Lower Addiscombe Road on overbridges. These bridges had been removed following closure of the line in 1983, as they were of sub-standard height and prevented modern double-deck bus operation. Rather than replace the bridges at a higher level and construct a stop to replace the original Bingham Road station, which would have been very difficult to make accessible for wheelchairs, it was decided to completely raze the embankments to ground level and provide a very convenient side platform stop between two new road level crossings. Earth noise bunds have been constructed alongside to provide noise protection. This stop is named Addiscombe rather than Bingham Road, to better reflect the district it serves, the original Addiscombe Station, 700 metres to the west, having closed in 1997.

After crossing Lower Addiscombe Road, the line rises up again to the original alignment and an emergency trailing crossover, but before long flattens out to approach the bridge under Blackhorse Lane. Before this, it passes the site of some demolished flats, only built after the original line was closed in 1983. A new stop has been constructed east of the Blackhorse Lane road bridge, accessed through former allotments.

The line then curves past the site of the junction with the former line to Addiscombe, closed in 1997, and after passing below a footbridge comes to Woodside stop, previously an imposing railway station. This was opened in 1871 to serve Croydon Racecourse and had very long side platforms with extensive canopies on both platforms and steps up to the booking hall over the tracks on the Spring Lane bridge. All of the track level infrastructure has been demolished and replaced by a standard side platform tram stop, but the station building remains and may be converted for retail purposes. Access is now by the original steps on the north side and a footpath to Spring Lane, near the bottom of its slope to the bridge.

Beckenham Road tram stop is fitted into an awkward site alongside a road overbridge. The ramp to the stop is behind the building on the right.

At Arena Junction, the tram is heading away from the camera and is about to cross on to the single line to Elmers End. The tracks curving to the left are the Beckenham line.

Beyond Blackhorse Lane stop the line curves at the site of the former junction with the line to Addiscombe.

A short straight section then brings the line to Arena stop, which is remote from roads but with footpaths going in several directions. The name refers to the adjacent Croydon Arena, an open air sports stadium. To the east of the stop is the last of the junctions on the system, a double-track crossing. The Elmers End spur continues straight on, following the former rail alignment. A short distance past the junction it becomes single track for the 700 metres to Elmers End. Approaching that station, the Connex South Eastern Hayes branch sweeps in from the right and straightens through the station. Just before the platform on the north-west side is a siding for use by spare trams. Trams use the former Addiscombe bay platform on the north side, allowing cross-platform interchange with trains towards Lewisham and London. As at Wimbledon, the track height has been raised on ballast to allow the original platform height to be retained. Passenger access is through the Connex booking hall.

Retracing the route back to Arena junction, the Beckenham route curves sharply to the left and rises up on to a new embankment across open ground, past the arena. As the ground level rises, the route enters a series of sweeping curves around the edge of South Norwood Country Park, passing a pitch-and-putt course on the right, which had to be partially resited during Tramlink construction. The line then crosses a private road into Beckenham Cemetery and enters Harrington Road stop, which lies alongside the rear of the cemetery. This appears to be an isolated spot, but the stop serves a heavily populated area some distance from existing public transport.

Addiscombe tram stop fits neatly between crossings of Lower Addiscombe Road and Bingham Road. This section was previously railway on embankment and bridges.

From the Harrington Road stop, the line starts to climb and soon becomes single track. A new sharply curved embankment had to be constructed here to bring Tramlink up alongside the Crystal Palace–Beckenham Junction rail line, whose alignment it shares for the remainder of the route. This alignment formerly carried two tracks but one has been sufficient for the half-hourly Connex service in recent years. The Tramlink single line occupies the southernmost side of the alignment and some slewing of the Railtrack line was necessary to accommodate it. The first stop on this section is at Birkbeck, where the disused up rail platform has been replaced by a single platform tram stop. This requires refurbishment of a disused staircase and a new footpath for wheelchair access to Elmers End Road, which has to dip down to pass beneath the rail bridge. Birkbeck rail station has a separate access on the north side of the bridge.

To gain access to the railway alignment near Birkbeck the Tramlink route curves round sharply, as seen in this view from the track before the curve has begun.

No.2530 at the rather cramped Beckenham Junction terminus, with the rail station in the background.

It is only a short distance to Avenue Road, which is a completely new stop serving closely packed Edwardian developments on both sides of the line for the first time. This is in a shallow cutting bridged by a footbridge, which remains. There is just enough width here to accommodate a passing loop and side platforms, accessed from Blandford Road. Cattle type grids are fitted at each end of the stop to ensure errant passengers do not stray onto the third rail electrified Railtrack line.

The land then falls away again to bring the line over Beckenham Road on an embankment and into the single platform stop of that name. This is in a restricted position and an elaborate zigzag path is necessary to reach road level by the underbridge. Unfortunately, there is not enough space to provide a loop at this point and it has been necessary to construct one a short distance further on behind houses in Thayers Farm Road. This was partly achieved by reducing the embankment height slightly and thus widening it. This loop is regularly used by trams passing as it is the last one before a long single track section to Beckenham Junction. After leaving the loop, the line sweeps gradually to the right and runs past the junction between the Crystal Palace and South Eastern main lines, from where a Eurostar train can often be seen pacing a tram into the station. All lines cross over the Mid Kent line to Hayes and the Chaffinch brook before passing another junction, with the spur from New Beckenham, shortly before Beckenham Junction.

Fitting Tramlink into Beckenham Junction was a far from easy task. It was not possible to find space within the existing rail station and it occupies a separate site, previously used as a bus stand, in the station forecourt area. To access this, the line has to squeeze past Dell Cottage, where clearances from the rail lines are at a minimum, then climb up a ramp behind a railway substation to reach road level. A two-track, island platform stop is provided, although normally only one tram is present.

Croydon–New Addington line

From Sandilands Junction, the curve to the south immediately brings the line into the first of the three contiguous tunnels taking the former Woodside–Selsdon railway beneath the hill crossed by Radcliffe Road and Park Hill Rise. The line is dead straight here and daylight can be seen through the tunnels. The tunnels, opened in 1885, were found to be in reasonably good condition and have been overhauled for their new purpose, including installation of lighting. Emerging from the south end of the tunnel, the trams follow a deep cutting which in the years of disuse became home to many badgers, whose welfare has been paramount through Tramlink's construction, to the extent of special 'runs' being built beneath the tracks for them. As the cutting fades away, the line crosses over Fairfield Path and passes through the site of the former Coombe Road station, partly used for new housing. The line then has to curve sharply round at ground level to run parallel to Coombe Road. To achieve this, it was necessary to demolish a small number of houses in Larcombe Close and Lloyd Park Avenue.

After crossing the latter road on the level, the line skirts Lloyd Park and reaches the stop of the same name, adjacent to the access road to the park's pavilion. As with all intermediate stops on this line, it has side platforms. A trailing crossover is situated beyond the road, intended for use when events are held in the park. The line continues through the park on ballasted track, protected by a low fence. From the eastern end of the park, the track starts to climb steadily, and enters the grounds of the eighteenth-century Geoffrey Harris House, and from here on, the landscape becomes heavily wooded. After crossing the driveway, the line runs through the beautiful Addington Hills and continues uphill, curving all the time, passing through and along a succession of cuttings and embankments, mostly away from the parallel Coombe Lane, with a maximum gradient of 8% being attained.

No.2547 approaches the top of the grade in Lodge Lane, New Addington, approaching the King Henry's Drive roundabout.

Above right At Larcombe Close, near Lloyd Park, a sharp curve is necessary for the transition from the former rail alignment to roadside reservation.

Right No.2546 amid autumnal splendour in Lloyd Park during October 1999.

When the line eventually flattens out again, it comes to Coombe Lane stop. This secluded stop is mainly intended for use by pupils at the nearby Royal Russell School and is adjacent to the now closed-off to traffic Sunken Lane. Soon after, the line passes a water tower on the left and crosses Coombe Lane near its junction with Shirley Hills Road. Originally, it was intended to avoid this busy junction by constructing a short tunnel beneath it, but a signalled level crossing was substituted as one of the measures to reduce the cost of the final scheme in order to obtain government approval.

On the south side of Coombe Lane, the grounds of Heathfield are entered; this is a landscaped garden containing many trees, bushes and shrubs, spectacularly set on a southward facing slope. Unavoidably, some trees had to be sacrificed to make room for the tram route which runs down a grade of 8% to reach fields alongside the busy Gravel Hill dual carriageway. In summer, these fields are busy with pick-your-own fruit customers. At the bottom of the hill, the line curves into Gravel Hill stop, which is adjacent to a housing area and school.

Crossing Gravel Hill on a skewed level crossing, protected by traffic signals, the line passes through a low cutting and curves into Addington Park. Here, it was necessary to resite a children's playground to make way for the tram route. A very sharp left hand curve brings the trams round into Kent Gate Way and past the realigned road entrance into the park. Kent Gate Way is also a busy dual carriageway and the tram route crosses first into the central reservation and then to the east side, by means of two traffic signal controlled skew angle crossings. This brings the line to Addington Village interchange where London Transport has constructed a new bus station to the left hand side of the stop. The interchange is a terminal point for feeder buses from New Addington and other surrounding areas. A trailing crossover is situated shortly after the stop to permit reversals here.

There are many attractive vistas on the New Addington route. No.2546 descends through Shirley Hills towards Lloyd Park.

No.2543 crosses Gravel Hill, Addington, heading towards Croydon on 17th September 1999.

In Kent Gate Way, there is a short section of central median strip, where the tram service curves against the curve of the road.

From Addington Village, the line sweeps round to the right to join Lodge Lane for the climb into New Addington and is on a roadside reservation for one kilometre. Lodge Lane forms the south western boundary of the built-up area of New Addington and a lot of effort was put into retaining as many as possible of the long line of distinctive trees that parallel the cycle track and footpath displaced by Tramlink. A stop is situated on this section, at Fieldway, and is also a major interchange point with local buses. At the end of Lodge Lane, the line crosses the large roundabout at the junction with King Henry's Drive and runs along the very wide central grass reservation of Parkway, passing through the King Henry's Drive stop shortly afterwards.

It is then a short distance to the health centre that blocks Parkway at its southern end and here the tram route has to squeeze round the building and is reduced to single track for the only time on this route. It then branches into two tracks once again, crosses a slip road and enters New Addington terminus. This is an island platform stop ending at the junction with Salcot Crescent and Central Parade, a short distance from New Addington's shopping centre.

Originally, the line would have continued alongside the west side of Central Parade to a terminal adjacent to the library and swimming pool, taking over a car park. This was another change made in order to reduce the level of grant required, and was judged to be unlikely to have much impact on passenger traffic.

At Addington Park, a sharp curve takes the line from Gravel Hill into Kent Gate Way. No.2541 is on its way to Addington.

Above Having left Addington Village and its bus interchange, No.2532 passes the crossover and starts to climb up the Lodge Lane side reservation.

Right The only single track section on the New Addington route is a short section past a health centre, immediately prior to the two track terminus.

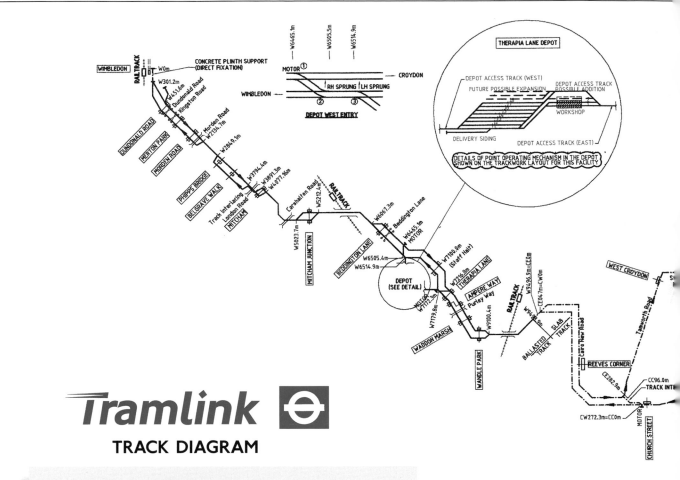

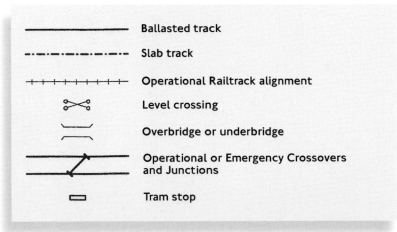

Tramlink ⊖

TRACK DIAGRAM

————————	Ballasted track
–·–·–·–·–·–	Slab track
+++++++++	Operational Railtrack alignment
⤬	Level crossing
‿‿	Overbridge or underbridge
⎯⎯⎯⎯⎯	Operational or Emergency Crossovers and Junctions
▭	Tram stop

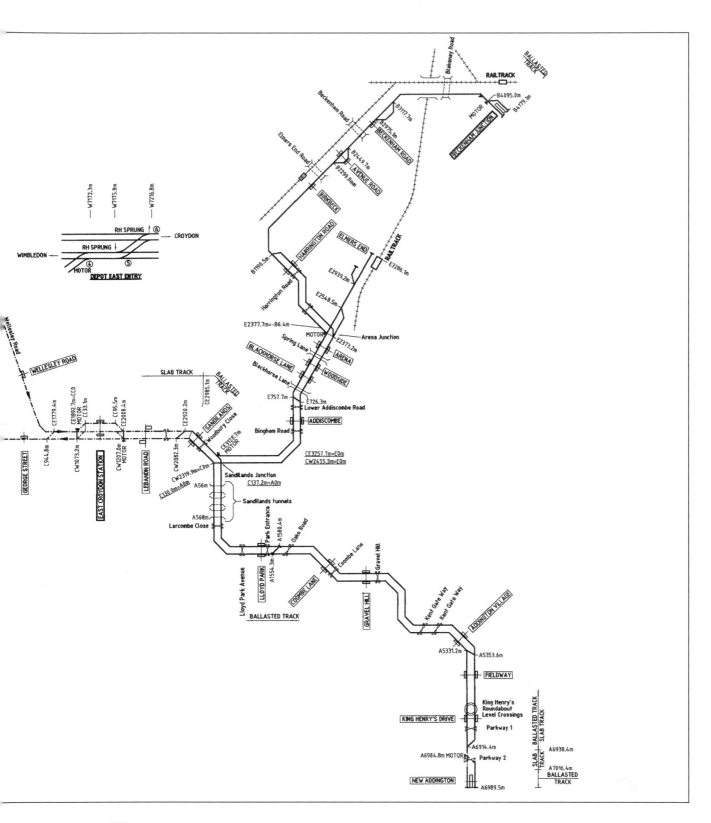

Tram 2540 in George Street approaches East Croydon station on the New Addington service.

TRAMLINK SERVICES

The shape of the Tramlink system, explained in the route description chapter, would in theory allow a number of different route patterns to be operated. However, the physical constraints of the system impose limitations on service design, and London Transport's minimum service level specification also has to be met. These also required that all four outer terminals must have through services to East Croydon.

TCL's initial intention was to provide a through Wimbledon–Croydon–Beckenham service to give the maximum number of orbital links between radial main rail lines. It would also have complied with LT's requirement for a daytime 10 minute frequency on both lines. However, this would have meant connecting together the two lines with most physical constraints, which are the two flyovers on the Wimbledon line, other single track sections on that line, and the long single track sections on the Beckenham line where it runs alongside Connex. It was concluded that there was some risk of the service being unreliable because of trams having to wait at passing loops on these sections, in addition to potential road traffic delays in central Croydon.

The short Elmers End line was only required to have a 15 minute daytime frequency, but Tramtrack's forecasts established that a 10 minute headway would be justifiable. It was therefore decided to propose a Wimbledon–Croydon–Elmers End route, which would have a much reduced risk of unreliability as trams would not need to pass on the Arena–Beckenham single track section. Therefore, this became route 1.

Traffic forecasts also showed that there was only a need for the 10 minute frequency west of Croydon town centre, and so with three lines running into the town from the east side, it was concluded that it would be best to terminate the Beckenham and New Addington services in the town centre. East Croydon station is short of the town centre from the east and is therefore not a suitable terminal for normal operation. The decision was taken that both routes should follow the one-way loop round the town centre to give excellent penetration and give a through service to and from West Croydon, which is not possible for trams going to Wimbledon.

Route 2 runs between Beckenham Junction and the central Croydon loop (tram destinations display West Croydon) every 10 minutes daytime and route 3 is New Addington–Central Croydon every 6/7 minutes daytime – this is also an increase above the minimum service level specification of 7/8 minutes.

The higher frequency of the New Addington line makes it difficult to link with other lines. The whole service would be too much for the Wimbledon line whilst half would be insufficient. Running one tram in three through (every 20 minutes) would require another route every 20 minutes from Elmers End to Wimbledon to interwork with it; it is felt by Tramtrack that a multiplicity of routes on lower frequencies would confuse customers and that it is best to concentrate on fewer higher frequency routes. Passengers are able to make a simple interchange.

In evenings and on Sundays the basic frequency is 30 minutes on routes 1 and 2, and 15 minutes on route 3. However, to give a better service to the Purley Way and Valley Park retail and leisure areas, route 2 is extended from central Croydon to Beddington Lane during these periods.

The normal daytime timetable requires eight trams in service on route 1, five on route 2 and eight on route 3, a total of 21 out of the fleet of 24. The full service runs from 7am to 7pm on Mondays to Fridays and during Saturday shopping hours. Lower frequencies apply at other times.

The concessionaire was required to say how it would provide an increase in capacity of 33%, if required, to cope with possible future passenger growth. There is scope for increasing frequencies throughout the system but, as an alternative, trams could be extended in length. In practice, it is likely that the need for increases will be on selected parts of the system and will most likely be met with frequency increases on specific routes.

This diagram illustrates the daytime frequencies (trams per hour) on each section, according to the width of the lines. The figures show the daytime trams per hour with the evening/Sunday levels in brackets.

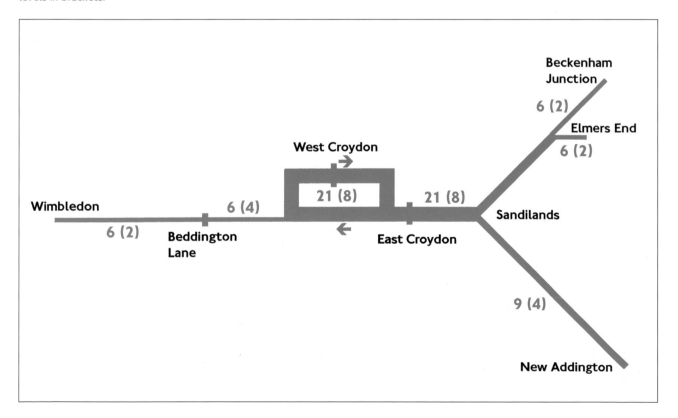

POWER SUPPLY SYSTEM

The Overhead Line Electrification (OHLE) provides the power to the trams and the rails provide the return path. The system operates at a nominal 750V DC with a peak power consumption of 1MW in any section. To provide power to the system 13 substations were built, each fed by a 6.6Kv or 11kV AC supply from the local Regional Electricity Company (REC) and equipped with transformer rectifiers of either 600kW or 1000kW capacity depending on location, to give the required output.

In addition to providing the supplies, one of the two RECs involved, Southeastern Electricity (Seeboard), were contracted to reinforce the local supply network to prevent unacceptable power fluctuations to Tramlink and the REC's existing customers.

Seeboard were also responsible for the detailed design and fit-out of the substations on the system. Each has a high voltage (REC) side and a traction power (Tramlink) side, with neither having access to the other. Intruder alarms are provided together with fire alarms, both of which are fed back to the Control Room using the Tramlink communications network. SCADA (see Control Command and Communications) is also provided to monitor the status of each substation. In an emergency, the substations can be switched out from the depot using the SCADA system.

From the substations the DC voltage is fed to nearby overhead line masts and connected to the OHLE wires. Each section of wire is double-end fed, meaning that there is a supply at each end of the section. This minimises voltage drop along a section and provides system robustness in the event that a substation has to be taken out of service. For maintenance and emergencies there are sub-section isolators built into the wire so that the shortest lengths possible are taken out of use enabling the system to continue to operate.

The majority of the OHLE masts are set into sockets. The sockets are generally in the top of a single bored pile. On the Birkbeck to Beckenham section, however, the proximity to the adjacent live railway precluded the use of the large diameter piling rig so mini-piles with a pile cap were used instead. In central Croydon mini-piles were again utilised but because of utilities many had to be hand dug gravity bases. With the exception of the socketed piles the masts are bolted down to the pile caps. In street the bolt heads are set below finished ground level to minimise impact on footways, but still allow replacement should a mast be struck.

The masts themselves are generally galvanised steel column H-section (RSCs) although a few in the vicinity of the Whitgift Hospital in the centre of Croydon are circular hollow sections (RHSs). Bracket arms are cantilevered to carry the contact wires from the masts with stay rods attached to them. In Croydon town centre, the use of 22 masts, mostly in George Street, was avoided by use of fixings on sufficiently strong buildings, together with span wires. This reduced the impact on the streetscape where the roads are at their narrowest and avoided the need for foundations in difficult locations. Elsewhere in the town, the number of poles on curves has been limited by use of span wires and bridles to control the wire as the alignment twists and turns through the streets.

The contact wire in fact consists of two 11.7mm diameter grooved section copper wires of inverted omega section on the main line to provide sufficient power capacity, but is a single wire in the depot and stabling area where current draw is lower. At its normal height of 5.8m, the OHLE is automatically tensioned by means of counterweights to minimise catenary sag. This design was chosen to avoid the need for more poles and the relocation of yet more statutory undertakers' services. The layout is designed such that with one pole removed the wire will remain above a height of 5.2m for road users' safety.

CONTROL AND COMMUNICATIONS

Most tram systems are driven by line of sight in much the same way as a road vehicle is driven. Signalling systems are, therefore, less important than on heavy rail installations where a train is driven in accordance with the signals. Nevertheless there are many places on the system where signals are required, such as road crossings and single line sections. For the latter, an automatic system is provided so that once a tram has entered a single line section from one direction, a stop signal is displayed at the approach at the other end of the section. There is also an emergency back-up alarm system.

Tramlink features a number of facilities for the convenience and safety of passengers including Passenger Help Points (PHPs), Passenger Information Displays (PIDs) and CCTV cameras.

The main tool for service regulation is the Tram Management System (TMS), a series of graphic screens showing the actual position of each tram against the schedule throughout the system, on a detailed plan of the track and signals layout. This data comes through the CCICS system, recording tram movements past transponder loops around the system. From Therapia Lane depot, the controller is able to control tram signals and initiate requests for traffic signal phases, if these are not obtained automatically by the trams. Radio contact with all trams is maintained utilising a touch screen computer for rapid set-up of calls.

The 13 substations are remotely monitored by the controllers at the depot using a Supervisory Control And Data Acquisition (SCADA) system. Through SCADA the controllers can, if necessary, isolate sections of the overhead line by switching off the power at the substations.

Tickets for the system are issued from machines located on each stop. These machines, supplied by Schlumberger, send passenger flow, various alarms and revenue information to the depot where a central computer logs the information and provides real time data to the controllers.

All of the above systems are fed along the Tramlink communications network. This is a wide band data-net the backbone of which is a fibre-optic cable running the length of the scheme. Intelligent Way Stations (IWSs) gather the information at nodes and send the data along the network to the depot where the signals are decoded and fed to the various computers used to manage the system. In the event that the network is damaged or the central computers fail, the system will continue in automatic mode as the IWSs do not require central instructions to function.

In the control room the various subsystems are displayed on monitors using the Control Centre Integrated Computer System (CCICS). This consists of three workstations which, using menu screens, can be used to examine or control any of the sub-systems above. Should there be an alarm anywhere on the system these are immediately brought to the attention of the controllers by the CCICS.

CCICS provides the means for the controllers to prevent bunching, feed in extra trams at peak times, react to incidents and emergencies, and generally monitor the tram system. With this system and the controllers skill it is expected that an efficient punctual service will be maintained under most operating conditions. CCICS, the communications network, the tram radio system, TMS and IWS were all provided and installed by Syseca Ltd.

TRAM STOPS AND TICKETING

East Croydon is the heart of the system and has three platforms, the centre one being bi-directional.

Tram stops are provided at 38 locations on the system. In street they are little more than raised footways with the front edge set 315mm above rail level. Off street they are miniature railway stations. All have a shelter with seating, a ticket machine, a passenger information point, CCTV camera, a help point and lighting; off-street stops also have bike racks. Only George Street and Reeves Corner have no shelters and seating. Shelters include illuminated advertising panels, except at Coombe Lane. The basic equipment is drawn from a family of standard components, supplied by Bus Shelters Ltd, as a kit of parts with the electronic equipment supplied by Schlumberger and Syseca. The extent of the equipment provided was determined by the anticipated patronage and available space at each location. The stops are designed for disabled use with the front edge very close to the threshold of the tram so that wheelchair users can access the vehicle unaided. Tactile paving and colour contrasts are used to aid the visually impaired. Ramps are provided to access the stops from roads or footpaths with slack gradients. The help points and CCTV cameras are provided to give security to Tramlink customers.

Tramlink is operated on an open boarding basis; that is, there is no ticket check as a passenger boards the tram. Every passenger is expected to have a valid ticket on boarding and for those who do not have a pre-purchased pass or concessionary ticket, it is necessary to purchase one from a ticket vending machine (TVM) situated at the tram stop. The system is backed up by frequent ticket checks and a high penalty fare, which increases if not paid quickly.

The standard Tramlink ticket machine is manufactured by Schlumberger in France and is operated by means of the black selector wheel with a central green button, located at the bottom right hand of the screen on which options are displayed.

The ticket machines are robust units derived from models already successfully deployed on similar systems in Europe. Supplied by Schlumberger, the machines accept a variety of notes as well as the usual coins and dispense change. Ticket selection is made using a menu driven screen and a selector wheel/button. Each machine provides a number of alarms, sent back to the depot over the fibre optic network, including 'being tampered with', 'out of tickets' and 'full' enabling effective servicing and maintenance of the machines.

DEPOT

The depot is situated on former rail sidings at Therapia Lane on the Wimbledon branch. The depot building provides four maintenance bays with associated equipment including hoists, an overhead crane, a wheel lathe and synchronised jacks for lifting a complete tram. In addition on the ground floor there are changing rooms and maintenance offices. Operating offices are on the first floor, including the main control room which is the nerve centre of the system.

Outside there are facilities to replenish the sand hoppers on the trams (sand is used to aid traction in slippery conditions or in emergency braking), and to wash the trams. At the western side of the complex are the stabling yards where all 24 vehicles are kept overnight.

In the design of the depot, provision has been made for a 33% increase in the fleet. As this could be done either by using longer trams or, more likely, by more trams, the depot can be extended in length or width. In addition more stabling can be added to the western yard.

The interior of the depot can undertake work on four trams simultaneously on its two tracks. Those at the western end feature high-level gantries for access to electrical equipment mounted on tram roofs.

The depot is located near Therapia Lane tram stop, with single track accesses at each end. The two-track depot building is viewed from the tram stop.

Trams are stabled in seven double-ended sidings at the western end of the depot site.

In the control room at Therapia Lane depot, a wide range of equipment and CCTV screens aid the controllers in running the operation.

Tramlink ⊖

When entering the depot from service, trams first have their sand supplies replenished from pumps.

Trams then move forward through an automatic washing machine before stabling in the sidings.

POTENTIAL FUTURE DEVELOPMENTS

Early amongst the plans was Merton Council's proposal for Merton Tramlink. This envisages an end-on extension from Wimbledon Station to form a loop rejoining the existing route at Mitcham Junction. The route would be about 6km long, partly alongside the existing Wimbledon–Tooting rail line as far as Haydons Road but then on street or across open land. It would mostly be single track due to width constraints. Tram stops would be provided at Haydons Road, Colliers Wood town centre, Lavender Avenue and Mitcham town centre. The service pattern operated would most likely be an extension of the service onwards from Wimbledon to terminate at Mitcham Junction, where a new turn-back siding might be necessary. Engineering and feasibility studies have been carried out, but no application has been made for Transport and Works Act approval.

To better serve the widespread retail warehouse park in the Purley Way area, a loop off the Wimbledon line has been the subject of study. This would probably leave the line near the Waddon Marsh stop and head westward across Purley Way. It would then turn north and pass the Valley Park multiplex cinema complex before turning east to rejoin the Wimbledon line near Ampere Way stop. The loop could be double track and might have junctions towards both Wimbledon and Croydon; however, a single track loop with a service to and from Croydon seems more likely if anything. No definite proposal had been announced by the time Tramlink opened.

Ever since the Crystal Palace was destroyed by fire in 1936, ideas for reusing the site on top of Sydenham Hill have surfaced at regular intervals. In 1998, proposals for a cinema and hotel complex were awarded planning permission by Bromley Council and attracted widespread local criticism because of access worries, including action by environmental protesters. At the same time, a study was planned to investigate ways in which Tramlink could be extended to serve the area. This mainly concentrated on considering several options for routeing, as there was no clear-cut choice. One plan would be to run on, or alongside, the existing Beckenham–Crystal Palace rail line, possibly accessing it by a westward junction from Tramlink north of Harrington road stop. Another routeing would be along the original South Met tram route via Anerley Road.

Whichever route is considered to be the best, one of the major issues is to find a way trams can reach Crystal Palace Parade, as the rail station (formerly referred to as the low-level station to distinguish it from the high-level station closed in 1954) is not near enough to the town centre. There are several options under consideration for this section. Firstly, a straight-forward extension up Anerley Hill, a drawback of which is the very steep intermediate gradient (although this was served by the original South Met route). The second option is a bus connection, either a dedicated bus or an extension of an existing route from the Parade to the Station. This is the least satisfactory option, as traffic congestion will not allow connections to be guaranteed. The third option under consideration is an escalator connection. This would have the advantage of running 24 hours a day and would be free. However, it is also probably the most expensive option.

Starting in 1996, London Transport carried out a series of studies into heavily used bus corridors in London that might prove to be the next step in developing tramways, although it was made clear that all modes would be considered and the title 'Intermediate modes' was adopted for the work. In the areas through which Tramlink operates, the main corridor studied was the north–south A23, once the trunk tram route to London.

Several other schemes for extending Tramlink have also been discussed, but little work has been carried out on any of them.